There is a Word!

GUIDEBOOK

Tyson Canty

COPYRIGHT NOTICE:

THIS DOCUMENT IS PROTECTED UNDER UNITED STATES INTERNATIONAL COPYRIGHT LAWS.

THIS DOCUMENT MAY NOT BE SHARED, MANIPULATED, COPIED, REPRODUCED, USED OR ALTERED IN ANY FORM OR BY ANY MEANS, INCLUDING MECHANICAL, ELECTRICAL, PHOTOCOPYING, OR OTHERWISE WITHOUT THE PERMISSION OF THE AUTHOR.

UNAUTHORIZED USE OF THIS DOCUMENT IS VIOLATION OF COPYRIGHT AND PUNISHABLE BY LAW.

Scripture taken from the NEW AMERICAN STANDARD BIBLE(R), Copyright (C) 1960,1962, 1963,1968,1971,1972,1973,1975,1977,1995 by The Lockman Foundation. Used by permission.

www.oneneighbor.net
ONE NEIGHBOR PUBLISHING LLC

INTRODUCTION

Welcome! This is the mini guide to the notebook, There is a Word! Bible Study Notes. Blank pages can be intimidating. If you read the introductory pages and looked at the sample Scripture notes, but are still hesitant to start, I hope this guide will get you excited and give you the confidence to put pen to paper as you dive into the pages of the Bible.

In There is a Word! Bible Study Notes, a list of helpful resources for personal Bible study and growth was compiled. The same list is below along with a detailed description of each resource to add to your studies:

2-3 Bible Translations
Strong's Concordance
Nelson's Complete Book of Bible Maps and Charts
Holman Bible Atlas
Nelson's New Illustrated Bible Manners and Customs

All the Names in the Bible (A to Z Series)
Merriam Webster Dictionary
The New Unger's Bible Dictionary

Bible Translations
When studying God's Word, it is important to have more than one translation open for comparison to ensure correct interpretation and greater understanding. Bibles fall in one of two categories: word-for-word and thought-for-thought.

Word-for-Word Bibles
When compared to the Dead Sea Scrolls, Word-for-word Bibles are 98% accurate. Word-for-word Bibles include King James Version (KJV), Amplified Bibles (AMP), Holman Christian Standard Bible (HCSB), New Revised Standard Version (NSRV), and New American Standard Bible (NASB).

Thought-for-Thought Bibles
The pros of using thought-for-thought Bibles are they are easy to read and understand. The cons are they lack in doctrinal reliability and attempt to interpret what the original author was trying to say. Thought-for-thought Bibles include Contemporary English Version (CEV), Common English Bible (CEB), Complete Jewish Bible (CJB), and New Living Translation (NLT).

The New International Version (NIV) is a cross between a word-for-word and thought-for-thought Bible.

Strong's Concordance
This is a giant index. It contains every word in the Bible of the specified translation. You can't use an New International Version concordance to find words in a King James Version bible.

How do you use a concordance? Let's say you are trying to find Psalm 34:8, "Taste and see that the LORD is good…" and you can only remember one word: taste. In the NIV Strong's concordance there are 17 Scripture locations with "taste". Look up each one until you find the Scripture you are looking for. Psalm 34:8 is fifth down in the list.

Nelson's Complete Book of Bible Maps and Charts
Bible maps are great for visually comparing distances and proximity between cities, towns, countries, and mapping various journeys, war campaigns, missionary trips, and much more. The charts included in this publication help with organizing timelines, comparing Scripture, and literary thematic structure of each book of the Bible.

Have you ever wondered where the locations were in the Song of Solomon? There is a map for that. What about the circular wandering path of the Israelites or the series of plagues that followed the capture of the ark of the covenant? There are maps for these as well. In way of charts, there is the contrast between the two Adams and another showing how the four gospels fit together giving events and scripture references. These examples barely scratch the surface of this exhaustive resource.

Holman's Bible Atlas
This helpful resource covers events from Genesis through Fourth Century A.D. There are 132 color maps paired with Scripture along with geological and historical information from biblical times. Use the atlas to quickly look up locations using the complete index. Over 100 photographs show how land mentioned in the biblical text looks today and any archaeological finds.

The New Bible Manners & Customs of Bible Times
Some of the actions and decisions made by those in the Scriptures may seem insignificant, but when the author makes mention it's a good idea to look further. Understanding the manners and customs

of the Bible is invaluable and can help paint a clearer picture.

For example, Matthew 9:1-8, the story of the man who was lowered through the roof by friends and positioned right in front of Jesus, brings to mind a few questions: 1) How did the men get their disabled friend on top of the roof? 2) What was the roof made of that made it possible to remove to lower the friend and not injure those inside the home? Towards the front of The New Manners & Customs of Bible Times by Ralph Gower, there is a full color illustration of a brick home. There are steps on the exterior of the home, leading from the ground to the roof. The roof was made of mud and wood beams. If the home in the story resembled the example, the men would have carried their friend up no more than twenty steps and removed a few beams, knocking a few patches of dried mud below to lower their friend into the home. How much richer does the story come to life with these added details?

All the Names in the Bible
There are hundreds of names in the Bible used for people, cities, mountains, rivers, nations, and locations for landmarks. Each name, believe it or not, means something. And if it's an Old Testament name chances are it's difficult to

pronounce at first glance. This helpful resource lists all the names used in the Bible in alphabetical order, with their meanings, pronunciation, descriptions, and Scripture locations.

One thing you may notice is the use of a name more than once. For example, if you look up Mizpah, you'll find it is used to name six different cities in the Old Testament and a little description for each. This information helps eliminate confusion when studying and you wonder if the authors are talking about the same location but got their coordinates wrong. Now you know there is more than one location with the same name and can study the correct description.

Merriam-Webster Dictionary
Regular English dictionaries are great for defining common words, such as, verbs, adjectives, and nouns without biblical connotation.

The New Unger's Bible Dictionary
The entries in this Bible dictionary give extensive descriptions, Scripture locations, and pronunciations where needed.

Let's say you are studying the armor of God found in Ephesians 6:10-17. There's the belt, breastplate, shoes, shield, sword, and helmet. In The New Unger's Bible Dictionary, you can read about the various offensive and defensive weapons, and you realize with the armor of God the only offensive weapon is the sword and the rest are defensive weapons. You also discover that it is the belt that holds the sword's sheath. Then the wheels start turning. If we are to put on the belt of truth first and the sword of the Spirit is one of the last things we are to pick up, there is a connection between truth and its necessity for properly carrying God's Word. There is so much more we could learn from the other verses.

Other resources
The list of resources given above is in no way an exhaustive list.

CHAPTER 1

In the following pages, we are going to do a sample study using There is a Word! Bible Study Notes. You will discover that sometimes even the smallest mention of a location, name, or cultural custom, can greatly impact and increase your understanding of the Scriptures.

First, set up the page how you want, filling in the Date, Scripture(s), and Message Title. Instead of Message Title, you can title your bible study if you would like.

This sample study will focus on John 12:23-24. Before you study your key scriptures, find out as much background information as possible. What leads up to your focus scriptures? If possible, write down the four Ws: who, what, when, and where. Record these under the main *Notes* section.

Who
Who is involved in these passages of Scripture? In verse 17, we read it was not just the disciples that traveled with Jesus from Bethany, but those who witnessed Jesus calling Lazarus from the tomb. There are also Greeks who are looking for Jesus in verse 20.

What
What is taking place? Jesus is traveling from Bethany to Jerusalem with an entourage. As Jesus enters Jerusalem, He is received with palm leaves laid at his feet. Greeks want to see Jesus. Jesus predicts his death and compares himself to a "kernel of wheat" (NIV) and "grain of wheat" (NASB).

When
In verse 1, we read these passages take place just before the Passover feast.

Where
John 12 begins in the city of Bethany where Mary, Martha, and Lazarus lived. Looking in the verses that follow, we discover in verse 12 the setting of our focus Scripture takes place in Jerusalem.

Notes:

Who: the disciples; those who witnessed Jesus calling Lazarus from the tomb; Greeks

What: Jesus is travelling from Bethany to Jerusalem with an entourage. As Jesus enters Jerusalem, He is received with palm leaves laid at his feet. Greeks want to see Jesus. <u>Jesus predicts his death and compares himself to a "kernel of wheat" (NIV) and "grain of wheat" (NASB).</u>

When: just before the Passover feast

Where: John 12 begins in the city of Bethany where Mary, Martha, and Lazarus lived. The setting of our focus Scriptures takes place in <u>Jerusalem</u>.

Record the meaning of "Jerusalem" in the *Words to define* section. It can be found in All the Names in the Bible.

Words to Define:
Jerusalem = "city of peace"

Using Holman's Bible Atlas, Bethany is shown to be 3 miles from Jerusalem. Record this information in the *Geography* section. To better visualize the distance, I found using Google that it takes about 20 minutes to walk one mile. Taking that in consideration the walk from Bethany to Jerusalem took about an hour.

> **Geography:**
> Bethany is 3 miles East of Jerusalem.

Place the two cities: Bethany and Jerusalem in the *Location* area.

> **Location:**
> Bethany - v. 1-11
> Jerusalem - v. 12-50

Look over everything that has been recorded so far. Then read John 12:1-24 again. The picture of what's taking place should be a little more clearer. You now have a glimpse of the key players involved, landscape, festive atmosphere, and underlying solemnity of Christ's approaching death.

In the next chapter we will fill out a few more sections and start to narrow in on the focus Scriptures.

CHAPTER 2

There is quite a bit happening in John 12, such as, the anointing of Jesus in preparation for His burial and Jesus' grand reception into Jerusalem, among others. However, to keep from gathering too much information that may lead you away from your topic of study, it is very important you stay focused. Jot down notes in the margins for future studies so you won't lose your thoughts.

To reign in our thoughts, remember our focus Scriptures are John 12:23-24. In the previous chapter, we recorded background information. What are some initial thoughts you have about the passages in general? Write them in the *Initial thoughts* section. I have written a couple.

> **Initial thoughts:**
> - Everything Jesus said and did was deliberate and intentional.

> • The "kernel of wheat"
> comparison was used with
> great thought.

Also, write down any questions you may have concerning the focus Scripture. For example, I want to know why Jesus compared Himself to a kernel of wheat.

Questions you have:
Why did Jesus compare Himself to a kernel of wheat?

To visualize a kernel of wheat, I sketched it in the *Sketch/Collage* section.

Sketch/Collage:

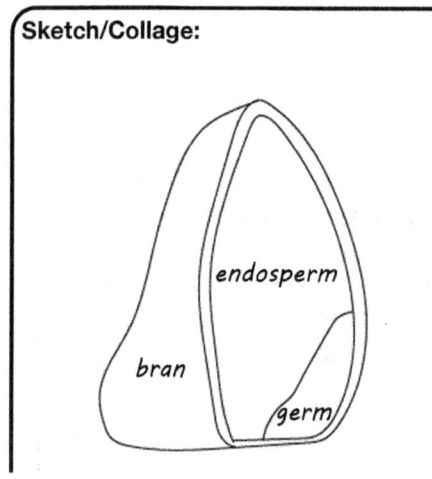

I briefly researched more about a kernel of wheat: the three parts and their purpose. In addition, I watched a time-lapse video of a kernel of wheat growing and recorded what I learned next to my sketch.

> *bran- outer covering of wheat kernel; source of fiber, heart and digestive health*
>
> *endosperm- food store for developing plant embryo; contains protein and starch*
>
> *germ- seed embryo*
>
> *Time-lapse video*
> - *roots grow first (radicle and adventitious roots)*
> - *single green shoot pushes toward surface (coleoptile - protects new leaves)*
> - *of soil is too warm, coleoptile doesn't reach surface and leaves don't either; climate is important*
> - *one seed can produce 8 or more heads with each head producing 40 or more seeds*

For this Scripture example, I am finished with the observation step of the inductive Bible study method (see **Crash Course in Hermeneutics** in There is a Word! Bible Study Notes). I did not fill in the *Implied* and *History* sections. In your own studies, you also may have sections without information. That's okay. You won't fill in every section every time.

CHAPTER 3

I hope you are feeling more comfortable about using There is a Word! Bible Study Notes. Each entry is four pages and we have completed the first three already. Keep in mind the second page is just extra space for notes.

We will now tackle the second step in inductive Bible Study, interpretation, to answer my question: Why did Jesus compare Himself to a kernel of wheat? This step needs to be approached with care. Set aside time for prayer as you seek the Lord to open up His Word to answer your questions. Your interpretation should *never* contradict God's Word. Look for other Scriptures to test against your findings. If there is no Scripture that supports your interpretation, it's safe to say you should keep studying and continue to seek the Holy Spirit for an accurate interpretation.

Scripture
Jesus replied, "Now the time has come for the Son

of Man to enter into his glory. I tell you the truth, unless a kernel of wheat is planted in the soil and dies, it remains alone. But its death will produce many new kernels—a plentiful harvest of new lives.

John 12:23-24 NASB

Overview
In John 12, all the events are leading up to Jesus's crucifixion and resurrection. We read Jesus is anointed in Bethany and welcomed on the road to Jerusalem with palm branches. In our key Scriptures Jesus is predicting His death, but there is deeper meaning.

Interpretation #1
In John 12:23, Jesus was saying that from His death, having fulfilled His purpose on earth, He will be exalted to a position of honor and magnified by the Father, not man (John 17:1-5). Jesus came to earth so that we might live through Him (1 John 4:9; John 3:16-17). The only way for us to have the opportunity of eternal life was for Jesus to die for our sins. It is through His death that His purpose was complete. Even on the cross Jesus said it was finished (John 19:30). One definition of Glory is the presence of God in the fullness of His attributes without diminishing His full deity. In John 17:5, Jesus prayed, "Now, Father,

glorify Me together with Yourself, with the glory which I had with You before the world was."

Interpretation #2
In John 12:24, Jesus compared Himself to a kernel of wheat to explain how His death was necessary and to what greater purpose it served. Without His death, there is no resurrection. Without His resurrection, there is no eternal life for those of us who call Him Lord. As long as a kernel of wheat stays on the stalk, it cannot be planted and grow into a thriving plant producing more seeds. It must be planted into the soil. From one kernel eight or more heads of wheat can spring forth each producing forty or more seeds. Likewise, from the death of Jesus Christ, His burial, and resurrection, men, women, and children that cannot be numbered have received eternal life. Christ was not just "planted" in a borrowed tomb but He went deeper and descended into Hades (Ephesians 4:9-10) to preach to those spirits of the days of old (2 Peter 3:18-20). He now holds the keys of death and Hell (Revelation 1:18). Without Jesus's death there would be no "plentiful harvest of new lives" (John 12:24).

Why did Jesus compare Himself to a kernel of wheat? It helped illustrate to people of an agricultural society the significance and necessity of His death in order to fulfill His purpose by providing a path to reconciliation for sinful man.

CHAPTER 4

We are now ready to move on the third step in inductive Bible study - application. The fourth page of the each study is dedicated to this purpose. The answers will vary for each person. It is a personal assessment of what you learned, how you can apply it to your life, and from your study what you would like to share with others. The last prompt is to end your study with prayer. You could pray for deeper understanding, boldness to share what you learned, and any other pressing circumstances relevant to one's daily life.

The importance of the notebook is to allow the Holy Spirit to speak to your mind and heart in order to deliver an authentic message from God void of fleshly motives. When this occurs, one's study becomes an active moment cultivating a deep connection and understanding of God's Word.

God's word never changes, yet He always provides

something fresh and new. No matter how many times you have read a Scripture or heard it preached, There is a Word!

APPENDIX

Page 1 of Example.

Bible Study & Sermon Notes

Date: 02/18/2020

Scripture(s): John 12:23-24

Message Title: Glory in a Kernel of Wheat

Notes:
Who: the discliples; those who witnessed Jesus calling Lazarus from the tomb; Greeks

What: Jesus is travelling from Bethany to Jerusalem with an entourage. As Jesus enters Jerusalem, He is received with palm leaves laid at his feet. Greeks want to see Jesus. <u>Jesus predicts his death and compares himself to a "kernel of wheat" (NIV) and "grain of wheat" (NASB).</u>

When: just before the Passover feast

Where: John 12 begins in the city of Bethany where Mary, Martha, and Lazarus lived. The setting of our focus Scriptures takes place in Jerusalem.

Words to Define:
Jerusalem = "city of peace"

Initial thoughts:
- Everything Jesus said and did was deliberate and intentional.

- The "kernel of wheat" comparison was used with great thought.

Questions you have:
Why did Jesus compare Himself to a kernel of wheat?

©2019 One Neighbor Publishing LLC

Page 3 of Example.

Geography:
Bethany is 3 miles East of Jerusalem.

Location:
Bethany - v. 1-11
Jerusalem - v. 12-50

Symbolism:
kernel of wheat?

Implied:

History:

Sketch/Collage:

(diagram of wheat kernel labeled: bran, endosperm, germ)

bran- outer covering of wheat kernal; source of fiber, heart and digestive health

endosperm- food store for developing plant embryo; contains protein and starch

germ- seed embryo

<u>Time-lapse video</u>
• roots grow first (radicle and adventitious roots)
• single green shoot pushes toward surface (coleoptile - protects new leaves)
• of soil is too warm, coleoptile doesn't reach surface and leaves don't either; climate is important
• one seed can produce 8 or more heads with each head producing 40 or more seeds

www.ingramcontent.com/pod-product-compliance
Lightning Source LLC
Chambersburg PA
CBHW071417290426
44108CB00014B/1866